Ladders

Rain Forest Animals

World Book

First published in the United States and Canada by
World Book Publishing
525 W. Monroe
Chicago, IL 60661
in association with Two-Can Publishing, Ltd.

For information on other World Book Products, call 1-800-255-1750, x 2238, or visit us at our Web site at http://www.worldbook.com

For information about sales to schools and libraries, call 1-800-975-3250.

Written by: Angela Wilkes
Story by: Belinda Webster
Consultant: Dr Sandra Knapp, Natural History Museum, London
Main illustrations: Steve Holmes
Computer illustrations: Jon Stuart
Editors: Sarah Levete and Julia Hillyard
Designers: Lisa Nutt and Alex Frampton
Managing editor: Deborah Kespert
Art director: Belinda Webster
Production manager: Adam Wilde
Picture researchers: Jenny West and Liz Eddison
U.S. editor: Sharon Nowakowski, World Book Publishing

Library of Congress Cataloging-in-Publication Data
Wilkes, Angela.
   Rain forest animals / [written by Angela Wilkes; story by Belinda Webster].
     p. cm.—(Ladders)
   Includes index.
Summary: Examines a variety of animals that live in the rain forest, including monkeys, sloths, bats, frogs, jaguars,
and snakes. Includes fact boxes and activities.
   ISBN 0-7166-7703-2 (hc). — ISBN 0-7166-7704-0 (sc)
   1. Rain forest animals Juvenile literature. [1. Rain forest animals.] I. Webster, Belinda. II. Title. III. Series.
QL112.W55   1999
591.734--dc21   99-13396

Photographic credits: p4: Planet Earth Pictures; p6: Bruce Coleman Ltd; p7: Oxford Scientific Films;
p8: Tony Stone Images; p9: Bruce Coleman Ltd; p11: Planet Earth Pictures; p14: Oxford Scientific Films;
p15: Bruce Coleman Ltd; p16: Oxford Scientific Films; p17: Bruce Coleman Ltd; p18: Oxford Scientific Films;
p21: Bruce Coleman Ltd; p22: Oxford Scientific Films.

Printed in Hong Kong by Wing King Tong

1 2 3 4 5 6 7 8 9 10 05 04 03 02 01 00 99 (hc)
1 2 3 4 5 6 7 8 9 10 05 04 03 02 01 00 99 (sc)

What's inside?

This book tells you about lots of exciting animals that live in the hot and steamy rain forests of South America. Some of the animals swing or fly through the trees, others roam the forest floor.

Monkey

Monkeys live in groups in the trees. They are amazing acrobats that leap from branch to branch and swing from the dangling vines. When monkeys play, they screech and whoop loudly. What a racket!

A monkey holds onto the branches with its strong **arms**.

Monkeys **chat** and squabble with each other. They also make funny faces.

A golden lion tamarin monkey has a shaggy golden coat. The fur around its face is so thick, you can't see its ears!

It's a fact!

Howler monkeys are the noisiest animals in the rain forest. You can hear their deafening howls miles away!

To keep steady, a monkey curls its long **tail** tightly around a branch.

Good **eyes** help a monkey spot danger and stay safe.

Monkeys have **thumbs**. Like yours, they are useful for grasping things.

Sloth

A sloth spends most of its life hanging upside down, fast asleep. When this strange-looking creature wakes up, it slowly crawls along its branch, looking for leaves to eat. About once a week, it creeps down the tree trunk to the ground.

A sloth hooks its three **claws** tightly over a branch, so that it doesn't fall.

A sloth crawls along the forest floor. It takes half an hour to move as far as you can walk in one minute!

Shaggy **hair** grows down from a sloth's body. This helps rain to run off easily.

A **baby sloth** clings to its mother's belly, where it is cozy and safe.

A sloth hardly ever washes! Green **slime** grows on its hair.

A sloth sleeps for up to 18 hours a day. It doesn't need to eat much food because it is hardly ever awake.

Bat

When night falls, bats wake up. They stretch their wings and leave their daytime resting places in trees and caves. Bats have excellent ears and eyes to help them find their way around in the dark.

Bats go to sleep hanging upside down. They fold their leathery wings across their furry body to stay warm.

A bat's hands are its **wings**. Its wings are covered by smooth stretchy skin.

A bat has a **furry body**. It is the only animal with fur that can fly.

This bat's large **ears** pick up sounds that even you cannot hear.

These baby tent bats snuggle up in a palm leaf. They will stay here until they are big enough to fly away.

A big **nose** sniffs out the ripest fruit and tastiest insects to eat.

Colorful birds

High up in the leafy trees, rainbow-colored birds sing and squawk. They swoop and climb through the trees looking for berries and nuts. You may even spot a macaw, one of the biggest birds in the rain forest, munching a tasty treat.

Colorful **markings** help macaws spot each other among the leaves.

It's a fact!

Hummingbirds are the smallest birds in the world. One kind is so tiny that it can perch on the tip of a pencil!

A macaw's waterproof **feathers** are similar to a raincoat. They keep out the pouring rain.

A strong, hooked **beak** is perfect for cracking open tough nuts to eat.

Sharp, curly claws, called **talons**, help a macaw grip branches or hold nuts.

A toucan's giant beak looks heavy, but it is hollow and light. It's made from the same material as your fingernails.

In the trees

The trees are packed with noisy animals playing and looking for food. Look at how they leap, climb, and fly!

How many tiny hummingbirds are flying around the flowers?

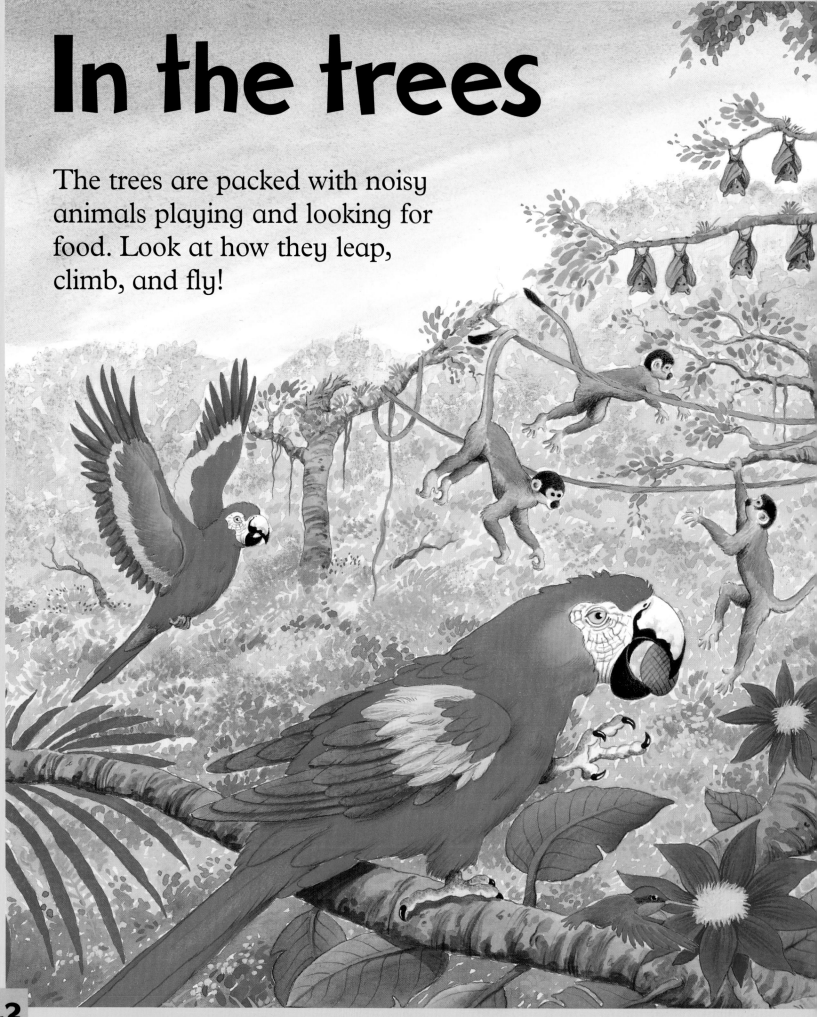

Which animal has green slime on its long, shaggy hair?

Which group of animals is hanging upside down fast asleep?

Words you know

Here are words that you read earlier in this book. Say them out loud, then find the things in the picture.

beak **claws** **thumbs**
wings **tail** **feathers**

What is the bright macaw doing with its sharp beak?

Frog

All kinds of brightly colored frogs leap around the steamy forest floor. They splash in rivers and make their homes in puddles left by the rain. The red-eyed tree frog in the big picture is an expert at climbing trees.

Two poison-arrow frogs crouch on a leaf. Their bright patterns warn hungry enemies that they are deadly poisonous.

A frog breathes through its **slimy skin**, as well as through its nose.

Strong back **legs** are useful for hopping after insects or springing away from enemies.

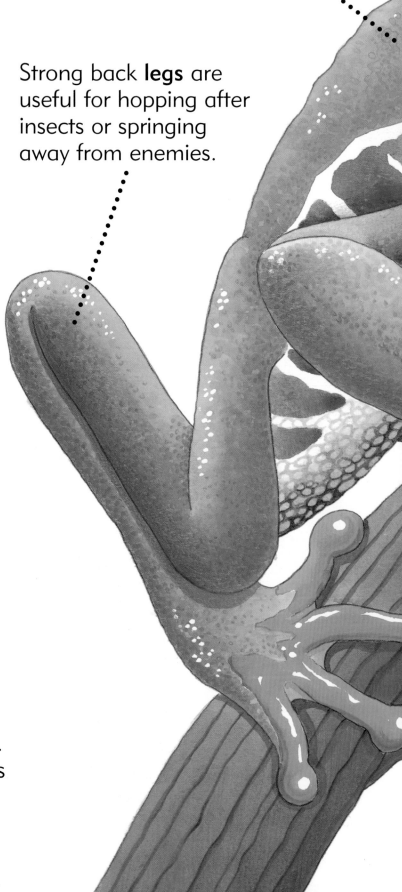

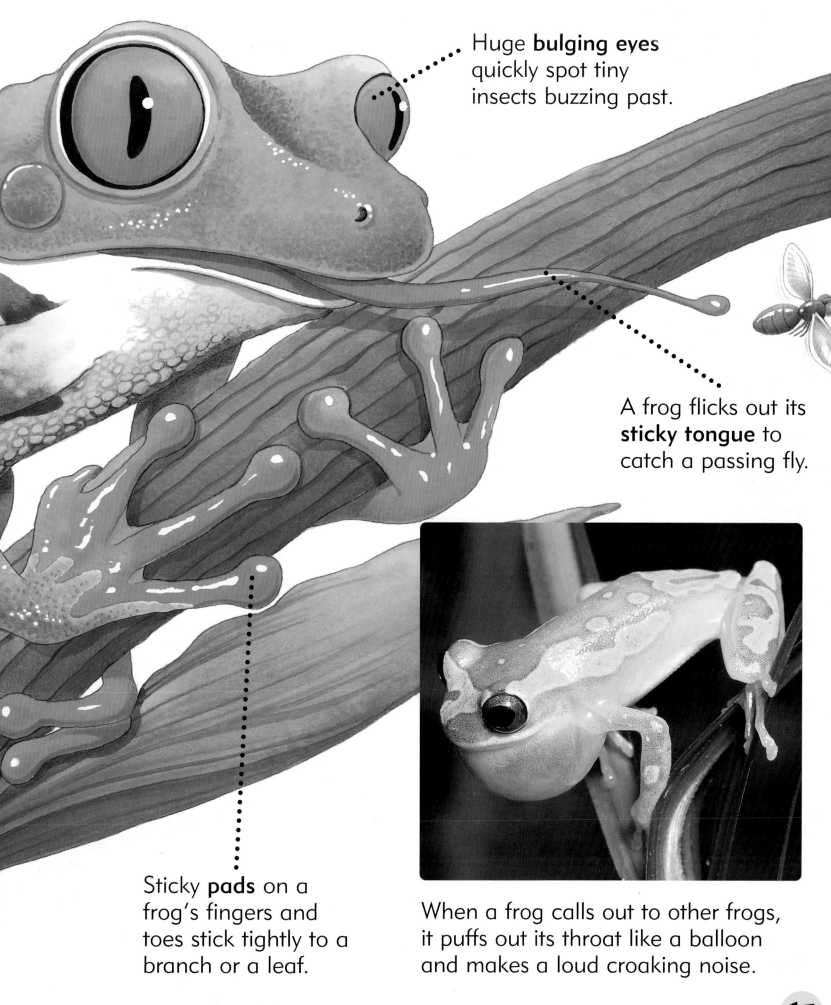

Huge **bulging eyes** quickly spot tiny insects buzzing past.

A frog flicks out its **sticky tongue** to catch a passing fly.

Sticky **pads** on a frog's fingers and toes stick tightly to a branch or a leaf.

When a frog calls out to other frogs, it puffs out its throat like a balloon and makes a loud croaking noise.

Jaguar

The jaguar is the biggest and most powerful cat in the rain forest. It can climb trees and swim after crocodiles. At night, the jaguar prowls the forest floor alone. Then it lies in wait for animals to eat. During the day, it relaxes in a tree or patch of grass.

Long **whiskers** help a jaguar feel its way through the thick grass.

Playing is a fun way for a young **cub** to learn how to fight and hunt.

A jaguar is a fierce hunter. When hungry, it creeps up on a small animal. Suddenly, it pounces before the animal can escape.

A spotted **coat** makes a jaguar hard to see in the shady grass and trees.

It's comfortable up here! A tree is a perfect place to lie in wait for a tasty meal or to take an afternoon nap.

Soft padded **paws** hide a jaguar's dangerous sharp claws.

Snake

Snakes slither across the dark forest floor and climb trees. The emerald tree boa in the big picture is hanging from a branch, ready to pounce on a tasty frog snack. After a really big meal, it may not eat again for a year!

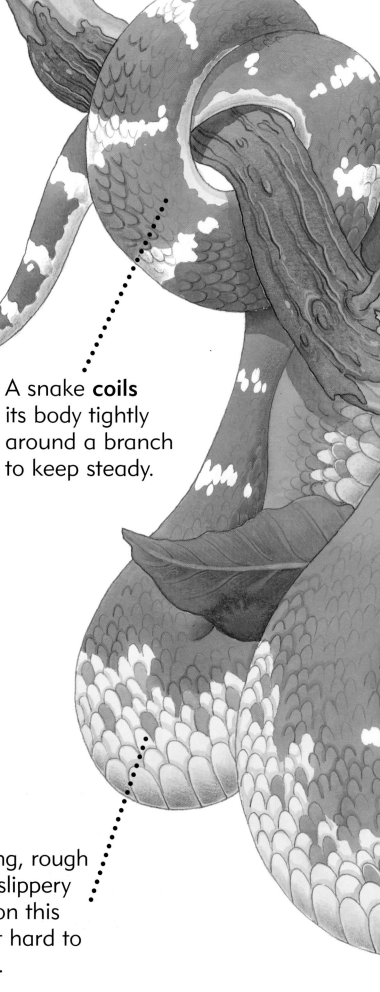

A snake **coils** its body tightly around a branch to keep steady.

This viper is about to attack. It will dart forward, then sink its fangs into its enemy.

As a snake moves along, rough **scales** help it grip the slippery branches. The colors on this snake's scales make it hard to see among the leaves.

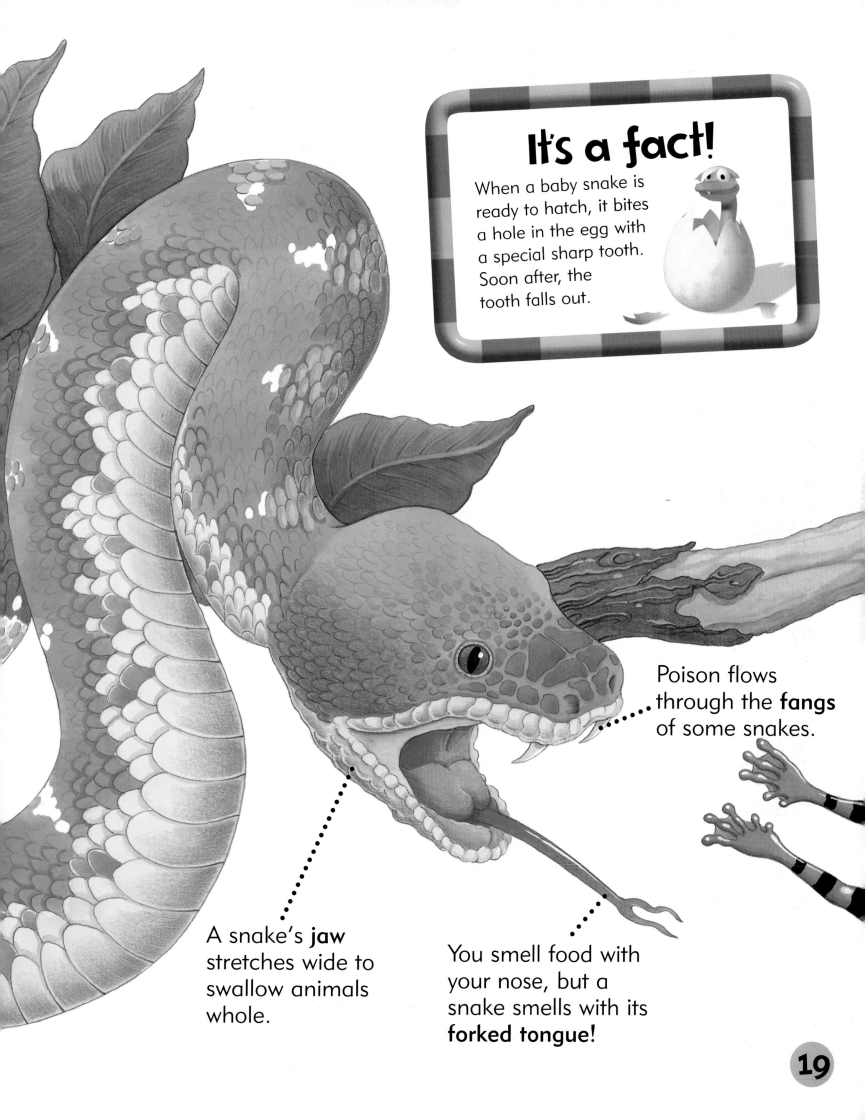

It's a fact!

When a baby snake is ready to hatch, it bites a hole in the egg with a special sharp tooth. Soon after, the tooth falls out.

Poison flows through the **fangs** of some snakes.

A snake's **jaw** stretches wide to swallow animals whole.

You smell food with your nose, but a snake smells with its **forked tongue!**

19

 # Crocodile

A crocodile spends the day lying lazily in the warm sunshine. In the evening, it floats silently in a cool river, keeping its eyes just above the water, on the lookout for its next meal.

It's a fact!

A baby crocodile is born on land. Its mother gently picks it up in her mouth and carries it safely to the river's edge.

When a crocodile dives, its **nostrils** shut tight to stop water from flowing in.

A crocodile's sharp **teeth** and strong jaws are perfect for snapping up tasty fish and even large animals.

A crocodile swims by swishing its long, **powerful tail** from side to side.

A crocodile waddles along the ground on short, **stocky legs**.

Webbed feet make it easier to walk on soft, muddy ground.

This crafty crocodile looks like a floating log covered in weeds. But watch out – with one swish of its tail, it will pounce!

Insects and spiders

There are more insects in the rain forest than any other animal. An insect has six legs and three main parts to its body, which has a tough covering. A spider has eight legs, fangs, and can spin silk. Spiders feed mostly on insects!

A **leafcutter ant** carries part of a leaf back to its nest to make food.

This shiny beetle hides among the leaves of plants, or burrows into woody stems, where it is safe from attackers.

A hard **case** protects the ant's body like a tough coat of armor.

A **butterfly** lands on a leaf to drink the sweet juice from a nearby flower.

Most butterflies have wings with beautiful **patterns**.

A butterfly's tongue is a long, hollow **tube**. It sucks up juice like a straw.

An ant smells, tastes, and touches the world around it with **feelers**. Most insects have feelers.

It's a fact!

There's a bird-eating spider that can be as big as a dinner plate!

23

The forest floor

On the dark, damp forest floor,
all kinds of animals are busy
hunting, playing, and looking
after their families.

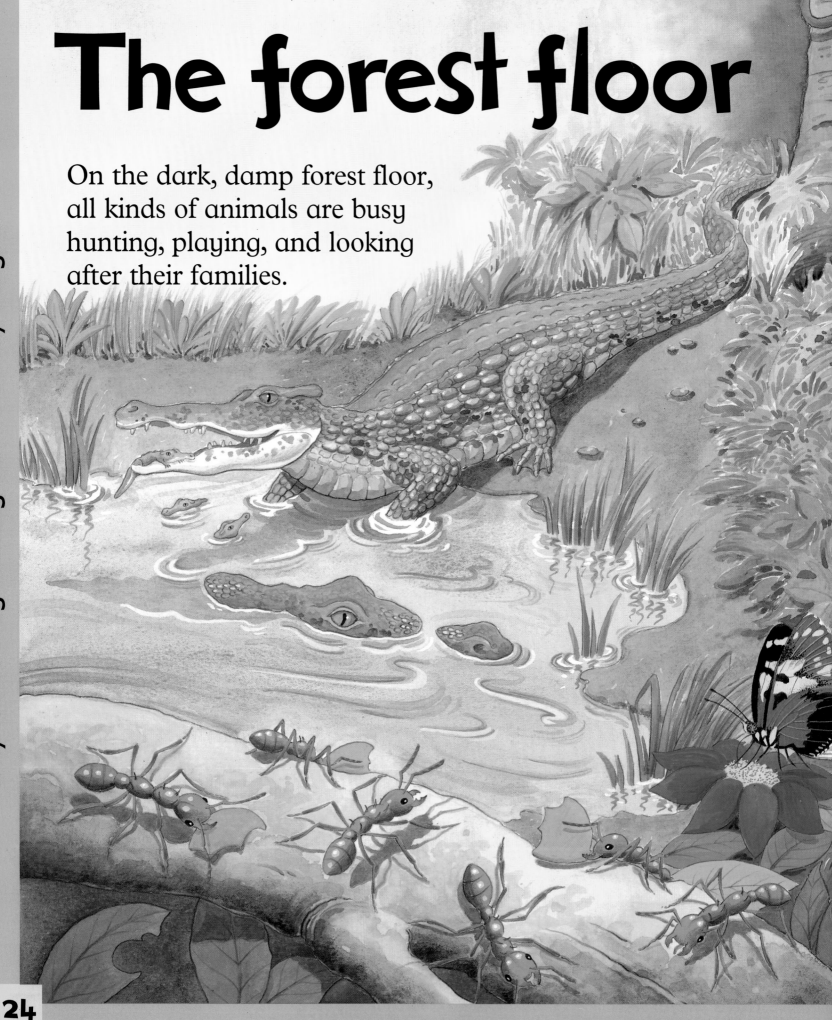

24

Words you know

Here are words that you read earlier in this book. Say them out loud, then find the things in the picture.

webbed feet	**paws**	**feelers**
forked tongue	**cub**	**pads**

How many ants are crawling along the log?

25

Message to the trees

Pitter, patter, splat. Pitter, patter, splat.
Frog woke up to berries landing on her head.
What a mess, squashed berries were everywhere.

"Not again," Frog muttered, looking up into the trees towering above her.

"Hey, you up there," she yelled, "stop dropping berries. Animals live down here you know!"

Nearby, Crocodile was basking in the warm sun. Plonk, splash, plop. Nuts rained onto the tip of his long nose.

"Ouch!" snapped Crocodile. "That hurt. Hey, you up there," he called, "stop dropping nuts. If you do that again, I'll gobble you up!"

Suddenly, in the bushes beside the river, "Aaaah-choooo!" Jaguar woke up with a loud sneeze. Something was tickling her nose. A beautiful red feather was tangled in her whiskers.

"Now where did that feather come from?" wondered Jaguar. "It must have floated down from the trees."

Jaguar could hear Frog and Crocodile complaining loudly.

"I was woken up again," croaked Frog. "Sticky berries are all over me. I look like blackberry jam."

"Another pile of nuts just hit me on the nose," added Crocodile. "I don't know where they keep coming from."

"Excuse me," interrupted Jaguar, popping out from the bushes. "I think I know who it might be."

"Who?" asked Frog and Crocodile.

"The animal who dropped this," replied Jaguar holding out the feather.

"If we find the owner of this feather, we can ask him or her to stop dropping food," said Frog.

"We must get a message up to the trees," said Crocodile.

So Frog and Crocodile wrote a letter kindly asking the owner of the feather to stop dropping food.

To the owner of the feather,

Please stop dropping your food. You are disturbing the animals who live below you on the forest floor.

Thank you,
from Frog and Crocodile

Jaguar took the letter and the feather and started to climb. Halfway up, she found Sloth snoring.

"Wake up, lazy-bones," whispered Jaguar. "I have something to show you."

Sloth opened the letter and read it. "The feather's not mine," yawned Sloth. "I have shaggy hair, and I never eat berries. I like only leaves. But I know who it might be. There's a little bat up above. She's always chewing fruit."

"I can't climb that high," explained Jaguar. "Will you take this letter?"

"Sure," sighed Sloth. "I haven't moved an inch today."

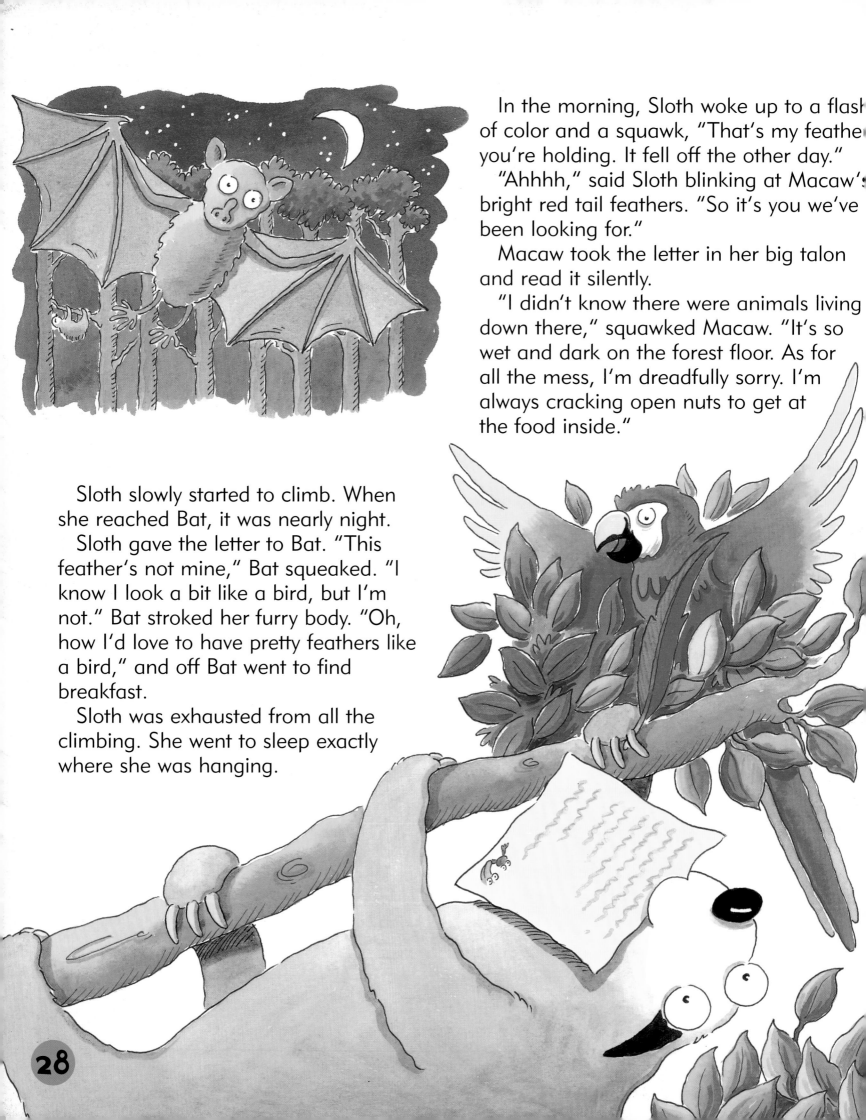

In the morning, Sloth woke up to a flash of color and a squawk, "That's my feather you're holding. It fell off the other day."

"Ahhhh," said Sloth blinking at Macaw's bright red tail feathers. "So it's you we've been looking for."

Macaw took the letter in her big talon and read it silently.

"I didn't know there were animals living down there," squawked Macaw. "It's so wet and dark on the forest floor. As for all the mess, I'm dreadfully sorry. I'm always cracking open nuts to get at the food inside."

Sloth slowly started to climb. When she reached Bat, it was nearly night.

Sloth gave the letter to Bat. "This feather's not mine," Bat squeaked. "I know I look a bit like a bird, but I'm not." Bat stroked her furry body. "Oh, how I'd love to have pretty feathers like a bird," and off Bat went to find breakfast.

Sloth was exhausted from all the climbing. She went to sleep exactly where she was hanging.

28

"Well," said Sloth, "You wouldn't want them coming up here and dropping food on you, would you? Can you imagine Crocodile swinging about up here with his sharp teeth and powerful tail?"

"Definitely not!" shrieked Macaw, trembling with fear. "Tell Frog and Crocodile I'll be very sensible from now on. I'll be careful where I drop my food."

Sloth slowly climbed back down to the forest floor. Frog, Crocodile, and Jaguar were waiting when she finally arrived.

"Did you find the animal who dropped the feather?" asked Jaguar.

"I certainly did," answered Sloth proudly. "It was a colorful Macaw. She was dreadfully sorry about dropping berries and nuts down here. She didn't think anyone lived on the forest floor."

"I hope she said she would stop dropping food on us," croaked Frog.

"Oh yes," grinned Sloth. "All I had to say was, 'how would you like it if Crocodile swung around up here with his sharp teeth and powerful tail?' She immediately promised to be more careful."

"Well done, Sloth," cheered Frog.

"But I can't climb trees," said Crocodile.

"I didn't tell her *that*," winked Sloth. "That's our secret!"

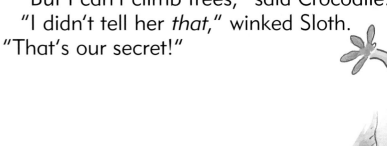